NORTH AND SOUTH

A TALE OF TWO HEMISPHERES

written and illustrated by

SANDRA MORRIS

CANDLEWICK PRESS

TO FELIX AND CASPER,
WHO LOVE ANIMALS
AS MUCH AS I DO

First US edition 2021
First published by Walker Books Australia 2021

Library of Congress Catalog Card Number pending
ISBN 978-1-5362-0459-9

TWP 25 24 23 22 21 20
10 9 8 7 6 5 4 3 2 1

Printed in Johor Bahru, Malaysia.

This book was typeset in Futura T, Kranky,
Stringbeans, Lore, and Perfect Day.
The illustrations were done in watercolor and salt.

Candlewick Press
99 Dover Street
Somerville, Massachusetts 02144

www.candlewick.com

AUTHOR'S NOTE ON ANIMAL LOCATIONS

A habitat for each animal in *North and South: A Tale of Two Hemispheres* is indicated alongside each animal's name, as well as on a mini map, to illustrate that animal's traits and behaviors in that hemisphere at a particular time of year. These animals may also live in many other places around the globe, and they may migrate across other habitats throughout the year.

Arctic Circle

Scandinavia

Sweden

Finland

Norway

United
Kingdom
Scotland
Wales
n Ireland
Ireland
England
Belgium
Germany
Switzerland
France

Denmark

Estonia
Latvia
Lithuania
Netherlands
Poland
Czechia
Slovakia
Ukraine
Austria
Hungary
Moldova
Slovenia
Romania
Croatia
Serbia
Italy
BiH
Bulgaria
Albania
Turkey

Eastern Europe

Belarus

Georgia

Armenia

Europe

Portugal
Spain

Cyprus
Greece
Lebanon
Israel

Syria

Russia

Kazakhstan

Mongolia

Uzbekistan

Turkmenistan

Kyrgyzstan

China

Asia

North Korea

South Korea

Japan

North
Pacific
Ocean

Morocco

Tunisia

Iraq
Jordan

Middle East

Iran

Afghanistan

Nepal

Pakistan

Taiwan

Algeria
Libya
Egypt

Saudi
Arabia

India

Bangla-
desh
Myanmar
Laos
Thailand
Cambodia
Vietnam
Malaysia
Singapore

Philippines

Oceania

Mauritania
Mali
Niger
Chad
Sudan

Oman
Yemen

Eritrea

egal
Guinea
ra Leone
Côte
d'Ivoire
Benin
Togo
Ghana
Nigeria
Burkina
Faso
Central
African
Republic
South
Sudan
Ethiopia
Cameroon
Uganda
Somalia

Sri Lanka

Indonesia

Papua New Guinea

Gabon
Congo
Dem. Rep.
of the
Congo
Kenya
Tanzania

Africa

Timor-Leste

Solomon Islands

Fiji

Malawi

New Caledonia

Angola
Zambia
Namibia
Zimbabwe
Botswana
Mozam-
bique

Madagascar

Australia

South
Atlantic
Ocean

South Africa

Australasia

New Zealand

Indian
Ocean

Antarctica

CONTENTS

INTRODUCTION

Earth is divided into the Northern Hemisphere and the Southern Hemisphere by an imaginary line called the equator.

One of the most important differences between the two hemispheres is the timing of seasons. Because of the hemispheres' different angles and distances relative to the sun over the course of a year, their seasons—and their weather patterns—occur at different times. In both hemispheres, animals deal with the changing seasons in various ways. Whichever hemisphere they live in, they need to be able to read the signs of the changing seasons to survive.

The rhythm of the seasons is being affected by the rapid heating up of our planet, caused by an increase in atmospheric greenhouse gases from human activities such as burning fossil fuels like coal and oil, deforestation, and agriculture and farmitng. Many species are now at risk. The oceans are warming, sea levels are rising, and habitats are disappearing. People's homes are also being threatened; some have been destroyed by extreme weather events.

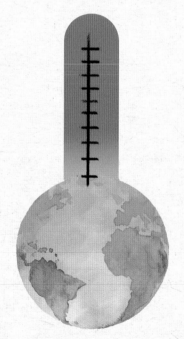

Warmer temperatures affect migratory habits of animals and insects and the sex of hatching reptiles. Habitat and food sources in some areas will be lost due to the changing conditions. Climate change is not the only thing affecting the future of our wildlife. Deforestation, poaching, and careless waste of plastics is causing dramatic loss of life for many species. It is estimated that sixty percent of mammal, bird, fish, and reptile populations have been wiped out since 1970.

CONSERVATION STATUS

(Based on the International Union for Conservation of Nature's Red List of Threatened Species, a trusted assessment of the conservation status of plant and animal species)

LC — Least concern: At relatively low risk of extinction

NT — Near threatened: Likely to become vulnerable in the near future

V — Vulnerable: At high risk of extinction in the wild

E — Endangered: At very high risk of extinction in the wild

CE — Critically endangered: At extremely high risk of extinction in the wild

	NORTHERN HEMISPHERE	SOUTHERN HEMISPHERE
WINTER	DECEMBER JANUARY FEBRUARY	JUNE JULY AUGUST
SPRING	MARCH APRIL MAY	SEPTEMBER OCTOBER NOVEMBER
SUMMER	JUNE JULY AUGUST	DECEMBER JANUARY FEBRUARY
FALL	SEPTEMBER OCTOBER NOVEMBER	MARCH APRIL MAY

In many tropical and subtropical regions, there are only two seasons—a wet season and a dry season. The incredible rainfall levels in the wet season are due to seasonal winds called monsoons. The "wettest place on Earth" is Mawsynram, India, which has recorded up to 700 inches (17,800 millimeters) of rain in some years.

	NORTHERN TROPICS	SOUTHERN TROPICS
DRY SEASON	DECEMBER JANUARY FEBRUARY	JUNE JULY AUGUST
WET SEASON	MARCH APRIL MAY	SEPTEMBER OCTOBER NOVEMBER

CUNNING CAMOUFLAGE

SCOTTISH PTARMIGAN & MOUNTAIN HARE

(SCOTTISH HIGHLANDS)

In warmer months, as ptarmigans prepare to breed, they make nests on the ground, sheltered and camouflaged near rocks. Their speckled black, gray, and brown feathers blend with the rocky landscape. As days become shorter, the ptarmigan begins to molt, and by winter its mostly white plumage matches the snow. In summer, the mountain hare's coat turns brown, helping it stay hidden in the summer vegetation. In winter, its coat will change to white to blend with the snowy landscape, keeping it safe from predators such as the golden eagle. A female gives birth to one to four babies—leverets—at a time, and she might have as many as three litters each year! Leverets are born out in the open. This is a dangerous time—nearby, hungry foxes, stoats, and weasels are always looking for a meal.

THREATS: Culling and loss of habitat

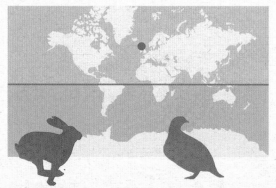

In winter, the Scottish ptarmigan's all-white plumage matches the snow, and in the spring, it molts to black, gray, and brown feathers that blend with the rocky landscape.

NORTHERN HEMISPHERE

The mountain hare's winter coat blends into the snowy landscape and keeps it safe from the sharp eyes of predators such as the golden eagle.

CONSERVATION STATUS: LC

For many animals, the most effective way to stay hidden from predators is to blend in with their background. Some animals even change their body color to match the changing colors of the seasons.

The green tree python mother guards her eggs, keeping them warm by coiling her body around them in her nest in a hollow tree. January marks the end of the mating season.

GREEN TREE PYTHON
(NORTHERN AUSTRALIA)

High up in the trees in northern Australia, green tree pythons spend most of their days curled around branches. At night, the python grabs prey with its large front teeth before suffocating it in its coiled body. From August to December, pythons mate and reproduce. The female makes a nest up in a tree or inside a tree hollow and lays six to thirty eggs. She then wraps herself around them to keep their temperature stable. Forty-five to fifty days after eggs are laid, bright-yellow babies emerge from their soft egg cases. The female leaves the nest to eat for the first time in two months. When they are between six and twelve months old, over several months or perhaps overnight, young pythons will change from yellow to green so they can remain hidden as they move deeper into the lush green rain forest.

THREAT: Smuggling for the pet trade

SOUTHERN HEMISPHERE

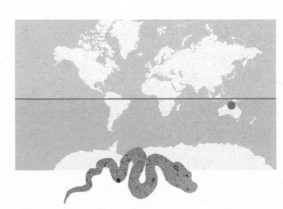

CONSERVATION STATUS: LC

FEBRUARY winter

JAPANESE MACAQUE

(JAPAN)

Fall to winter (September to April) is the main breeding season for most macaques (also known as "snow monkeys") in Japan. During this time, some northernmost troops migrate to sheltered valleys to avoid the deeper snow up in the mountains, while others stay warm by sitting in hot springs. Troops number on average around forty individuals. In the fall, macaques prepare for the lean winter ahead and feed on lots of fruit and nuts. In winter, if food is scarce, some macaques will dig up roots and catch fish. In spring, there is an abundance of new leaves to eat, and the females give birth to a single baby. At somewhere between eight months and two-and-a-half years old, the young macaques stop nursing but stay near their mothers for comfort and transport. When they are a little older, they join groups of other juveniles.

THREATS: Deforestation and human settlement

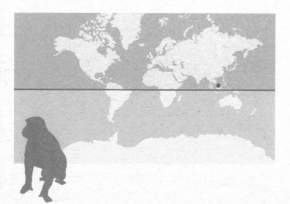

Soaking up the warmth in the Jigokudani thermal pools is one answer to the cold and snow for some Japanese macaques.

NORTHERN HEMISPHERE

CONSERVATION STATUS: **LC**

Animals that make their homes in extreme conditions have had to come up with their own ways of surviving, sometimes through special behaviors and sometimes through changes in their physical features.

LESSER FLAMINGO

(TANZANIA, AFRICA)

SOUTHERN HEMISPHERE

All year round, flamingos sieve food (algae and shrimp containing pink pigment, and fly larvae) through their beaks from African soda lakes. After about two years, the pink pigment gives the flamingo its distinctive pink plumage and it is ready to breed. Courtship displays are most common between October and February. Mating pairs build nests high on shorelines, clear of the season's rising water levels. Breeding occurs mostly just after the rains in May. Both parents take turns sitting on the single egg for a month, and they will both feed the chick, once hatched, for a week with regurgitated "red milk." After about three weeks, chicks are old enough to leave the nest and join thousands of other young flamingos, forming large crèches of gray birds. At three or four months old, chicks join the huge adult flock, searching nightly for the best feeding grounds.

THREAT: Global warming affecting food supply and breeding

In summer, flamingo chicks gather in large crèches on Lake Natron, a soda lake in Tanzania, where both parents feed them "red milk" produced by glands in their digestive tracts.

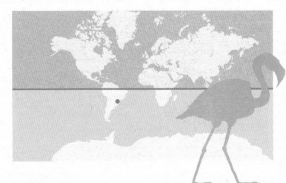

CONSERVATION STATUS: V

MOTHERS AND BABIES

POLAR BEAR
(THE ARCTIC CIRCLE)

A pregnant polar bear spends winter in a snow den, giving birth there in December or January, usually to two cubs. The family stays in the den until spring, the cubs nursing and Mom surviving on her own fat reserves. Some polar bears wander inland to eat berries and grass, but most journey to the sea ice, where they hunt for seals. Because of warming seas and melting sea ice, polar bears need to swim and walk farther for a meal. This means they burn through energy far more quickly than usual, losing weight and muscle and, sometimes, starving to death. Cubs nurse for at least twenty months and stay with their mom for up to three years. Females will be ready to breed at around four years of age, males between six and ten. Females only mate when they aren't caring for cubs—about every three years. In the fall, they eat as much as possible while migrating back to their winter habitats, and pregnant females make their snow dens for winter.

THREAT: Climate change causing loss of habitat

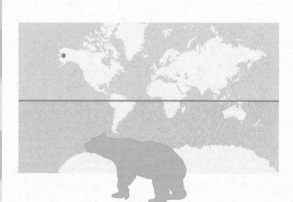

MARCH
spring

The warm Arctic spring in Alaska brings the mother polar bear and her two cubs out from their snow den.

NORTHERN HEMISPHERE

CONSERVATION STATUS: V

All over the globe, animals are creating families. Mothers treasure and protect their babies and have different ways of introducing them to the world.

SOUTHERN HEMISPHERE

Australia's saltwater crocodiles breed during the wet season (November to March), with a female laying between forty and sixty eggs that she guards for up to three months.

SALTWATER CROCODILE
(NORTHERN AUSTRALIA)

Measuring up to 20 feet (6 meters), this is the largest of all reptiles. After mating, female crocodiles make a nest of mud and vegetation and lay between forty and sixty eggs. Hatchlings have the best chance of survival in the wet season when there are plenty of aquatic insects, tadpoles, and small fish to eat. If the temperature in the mud nest is 82–86°F (28–30°C), hatchlings will be female, and if it is 86–89.6°F (30–32°C), they will be male. When a mother hears her young yelping inside the mud nest, she digs them out and carries them gently in her jaws down to the river. Only 1 percent of hatchlings make it to adulthood. The young are very aggressive toward one another and can also be eaten by goannas, barramundi, and other larger crocodiles.

THREAT: Habitat destruction due to human settlement

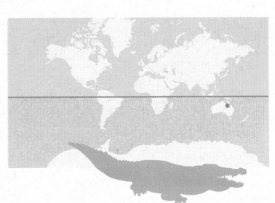

CONSERVATION STATUS: LC

BUILDING A HOME

AMERICAN BEAVER
(NORTH AMERICA)

Beaver family members gather sticks, logs, and tree trunks to build dams around their lodges to protect them from predators such as mountain lions, bears, lynx, wolverines, and coyotes. In winter, beavers largely stay in their lodges, feeding on food stores they have cached below the ice. When the spring thaw begins, the beavers emerge to make repairs to their lodges and dams. They no longer rely on their food stores and now eat fresh vegetation. The female gives birth to up to six baby beavers—kits—in late spring or early summer. All members of the family collect vegetation for the kits to eat. After a month, the kits emerge from the lodge for the first time and are watched over by the whole family. After about two years, the kits are ready to leave home.

THREATS: Hunting and trapping

The spring thaw has damaged the beaver lodge, and now it is time to repair it to keep the family safe from predators.

NORTHERN HEMISPHERE

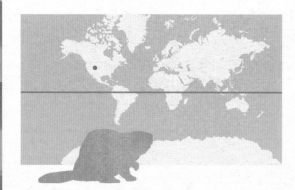

CONSERVATION STATUS: LC

Some animals are more creative than others in using the resources available to them to construct homes to protect themselves and their babies from the elements and from predators.

SOUTHERN HEMISPHERE

In South American swamp areas, hoatzins battle for nest sites over the river.

HOATZIN

(AMAZON RIVER, SOUTH AMERICA)

In April, the rivers rise in the Amazon basin and flocks of hoatzins split into small breeding pairs, jostling for the best sites over the waters to build nest platforms made from twigs. Females lay two to three eggs, and other group members assist with incubation for about four weeks. Hatchlings are fed regurgitated fermented plants. If in danger, the young birds jump into the river below, and when the coast is clear, they haul themselves back up the branches using their beaks and specialized claws on their wings. They will lose these claws as adults. When not breeding, hoatzins forage in colonies of typically ten to fifty birds, eating leaves, buds, and roots. Hoatzins have digestive systems similar to those in cows. They are also known as stink birds and emit a smell like manure. This smell attracts capuchin monkeys, as well as snakes and other birds, who prey on the chicks.

THREAT: Habitat destruction due to human settlement

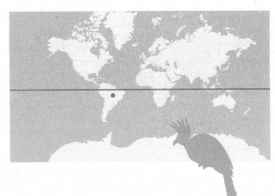

CONSERVATION STATUS: LC

SHOWING OFF

BLUE-FOOTED BOOBY

(TROPICAL & SUBTROPICAL PACIFIC ISLANDS)

There are about forty thousand breeding pairs of blue-footed boobies in the world. Their natural habitat extends from islands in the Gulf of California (in the Northern Hemisphere) down to Peru (in the Southern Hemisphere). They are spectacular divers and capture their main food source, fish, this way. They are very sociable and are often seen in flocks of up to two hundred. Most of their lives are spent at sea, but they come ashore to breed. Mating season usually begins in May and is the best time to see the male perform his striking courtship display. After mating, the female will lay up to three blue eggs onto the bare ground. Once the blue-footed booby chicks have hatched, the male brings back food for the female and the chicks. The parents feed chicks regurgitated fish from their bills. After two months, the chicks are ready to leave their parents.

THREATS: Habitat loss and egg collecting

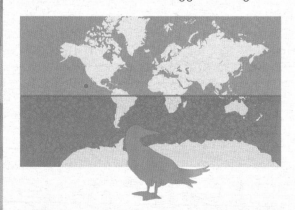

With his beautiful bright-blue feet, the blue-footed booby steps, struts, stomps, and, pointing his bill skyward, makes high-pitched whistles.

NORTHERN HEMISPHERE

CONSERVATION STATUS: LC

Putting on a show-and-dance performance is one way animals attract their mates. Some performances are very creative and can involve a lot of fancy footwork, while other performances rely on displaying beautiful features.

Shimmying his elegant tail feathers over his head, the male lyrebird of Australia is out to impress a mate.

SOUTHERN HEMISPHERE

LYREBIRD
(AUSTRALIA)

Male lyrebirds are famous for their ability to mimic anything from other bird calls to chainsaws to mobile phones. From May to August, males stand on their courtship mounds, spreading their beautiful long tails over their heads. The tails, which they develop when they are three or four years old, are dark brown on top and silver underneath and resemble a lyre (an ancient Greek musical instrument) when fanned out. The male shimmies his feathers and sings for up to twenty minutes to attract a number of female mates. The female builds a dome-shaped nest of sticks and lines it with ferns, feathers, and mosses. Her one egg hatches in spring, and her chick will remain in the nest for six to ten weeks. She incubates and raises the chick alone. Females start breeding at five to six years of age and males at six to eight years.

THREATS: Habitat loss and egg collecting

MAY fall

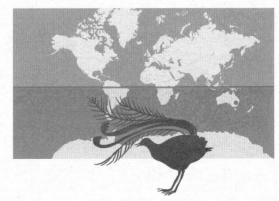

CONSERVATION STATUS: LC

ARMORED ANIMALS

STAG BEETLE

(EUROPE)

After mating, the female stag beetle burrows into rotting wood or soil to lay up to twenty-one eggs. In the fall, the adults will die, the eggs will hatch, and the brown and white larvae feed on the rotten wood. They may stay there for three to seven years, protected from winter weather, before building a cocoon and developing into adults. In May, after fully grown larvae have laid their cocoons in soil or rotting wood, the adult stag beetle emerges. In the evenings, the male flies off to find a mate before he dies in August. With his stag-like jaws and hard exoskeleton protecting his soft body underneath, he must battle with other males to win her. Adult stag beetles do not eat and instead live off the food reserves they built up as larvae, as well as sap or juice from fallen fruits that they lick up with their feathery tongues.

THREATS: Loss of habitat and predators such as crows, cats, foxes, and kestrels

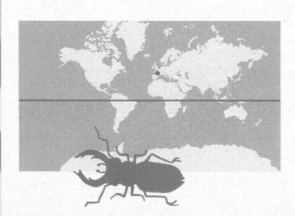

Fighting with their enormous jaws, male stag beetles battle each other to win the right to mate with a female.

NORTHERN HEMISPHERE

CONSERVATION STATUS: NT

Many creatures require tough exoskeletons, shells, or carapaces to protect them from predators, battles with rivals, or even their environment.

SOUTHERN HEMISPHERE

Female leatherback turtles come ashore on special nights to lay their eggs on sandy beaches in Papua New Guinea, the Solomon Islands, and the Florida coast.

LEATHERBACK TURTLE
(PACIFIC, ATLANTIC & INDIAN OCEANS)

Leatherback turtles are protected by a bony plate under their skin, hence the name "leatherback." They live in many oceans, as far north as Alaska and as far south as the Cape of Good Hope, and spend most of their lives at sea, eating mainly jellyfish. A pregnant female makes a long migratory journey to nest on sandy beaches in tropical latitudes, including in Papua New Guinea, the Solomon Islands, and the Florida coast. She hauls herself up the beach, scrapes out a nest in the sand, and lays an average of eighty to eighty-five eggs before returning to the ocean. Sand temperatures below 84°F (28.75°C) will produce male offspring; temperatures above 85.5°F (29.75°C) will produce females. By June, the leatherback's nesting season is almost over. After about sixty days, hatchlings break through the sand and race to the ocean. Only one in a thousand will survive to adulthood.

THREATS: Loss of habitat, hunting, changing temperatures, marine debris

JUNE winter

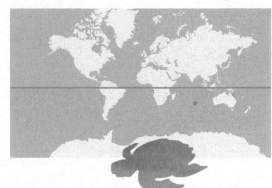

CONSERVATION STATUS: V

GRIZZLY BEAR
(ALASKA)

In late July, Alaskan grizzlies begin hungrily feasting on salmon starting to congregate in river mouths. Some large males can catch as many as thirty salmon in a day. At this time of year, berries, wildflowers, fungi, forest fruits, small mammals, and wild honey are plentiful. In a few months, grizzlies will have stored enough fat to hibernate all winter. Their heart rate drops and their body temperature falls to conserve energy. During January or February, female grizzlies give birth, usually to two cubs. By July, the cubs are four months old and are very boisterous and inquisitive. They learn what to eat by copying their mothers. Cubs become independent at two to three years. Young males will travel to find a new territory while young females generally stay near their mother's territory. A few weeks after her cubs leave, the female will mate again.

THREATS: Global warming affecting food sources; human contact

NORTHERN HEMISPHERE

Catching a ride on Mom's back is the perfect way for the young eastern quoll to join in the nightly hunt for food.

CONSERVATION STATUS: LC

Animals that don't migrate or hibernate gather food to store in their burrows and dens or hunt for as much as they can when food is plentiful to build up body fat.

In Alaska's rivers, a multitude of salmon swim upstream as grizzly bears wait patiently on ledges for a ready meal.

SOUTHERN HEMISPHERE

EASTERN QUOLL
(TASMANIA)

Eastern quolls are mainly found in Tasmania, Australia, although in 2019 they were translocated to several mainland sites. During the day, quolls sleep in dens made of rocks, or in tree hollows, and they feed mainly on small birds, lizards, and insects at night. In the fall, they also feed on fruits and start competing for mates. In winter, females give birth to as many as thirty young, each the size of a grain of rice. The first six to attach to her teats in her fur-lined pouch will survive. They remain in the pouch for up to two months, developing fur and eventually opening their eyes. After about ten weeks, their mother places them in a grass-lined den while she hunts and forages. By late winter they are able to play outside the den and travel on their mother's back when she hunts at night. By late November the young are weaned and become independent.

THREATS: Feral predators such as cats and foxes

JULY winter

CONSERVATION STATUS: E

FEISTY FATHERS

CARIBOU
(ALASKA, UNITED STATES)

In spring, caribou migrate north into the tundra where the snow has thawed and plants bloom. Calves are born and within two hours they can walk. In two months, they will stop feeding from their mothers. In August, caribou herds are completing their summer migration, feeding on tundra grasses. The males shed their antler fur in preparation for sparring and rutting (breeding). By September, fighting begins, becoming more frequent toward October as rutting starts. Males fight fiercely for the right to mate with females. In winter, caribou dig deep in the snow for moss and lichen to feed on. Their coat is now whiter. They then start to migrate south to avoid the Arctic winter and travel up to 50 miles (80 kilometers) a day, usually along the same pathways used by generations of caribou.

THREATS: Climate change is creating irregular winter icing events and an increase in biting flies in summer, affecting access to grazing lands.

At the end of the Arctic summer, the Alaskan tundra is alive with the sound of clashing antlers. The male caribou are sparring to win a mate.

NORTHERN HEMISPHERE

Sitting on a huge egg is not easy, but the male brown kiwi of New Zealand is responsible for keeping it warm until it hatches.

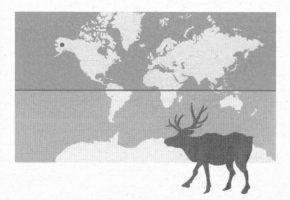

CONSERVATION STATUS: V

With the changing seasons and changing temperatures, male animals are involved in mating rituals and breeding, and some even take on the role of dad solo.

SOUTHERN HEMISPHERE

BROWN KIWI
(NEW ZEALAND)

The flightless brown kiwi mates for life. The female usually produces only one egg per year, which weighs on average one-fifth of her body mass. Her mate incubates it for eleven weeks inside a warm burrow camouflaged with sticks and leaves. At night he leaves the burrow to eat, hiding the entrance again. Between August and April, the chick breaks out of the egg using its bill and by kicking with its strong legs. For the first few days it feeds off the yolk in its belly. When it is between six and ten days old, the chick emerges from the burrow to forage on vegetation. Its bill is too soft to probe soil, but as it grows it uses its nostrils to find prey and feeds on spiders, worms, beetles, insect larvae, seeds, and fruit. Brown kiwis usually leave their parents' territory after about four to six weeks. Only about five percent of chicks survive to adulthood in the wild.

THREATS: *Predation by dogs, cats, stoats, and other animals*

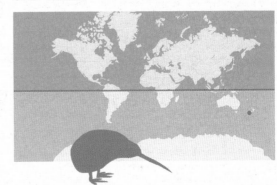

CONSERVATION STATUS: V

A NUMBERS GAME

PORTUGUESE MAN-OF-WAR

(PACIFIC, CARIBBEAN, INDIAN, AND ATLANTIC OCEANS)

The Portuguese man-of-war is not really a jellyfish. It is a colony of small animals called polyps that need one another to survive. There are four different types of polyps within a single colony. One type forms the float, which is full of gas. It sits above the water and resembles a Portuguese warship. Others form the long trailing tentacles that are armed with a poison that paralyzes then kills small fish prey. Another polyp contains the digestive organisms. There is also a breeding polyp that may release masses of reproductive cells into the tropical and subtropical waters at any time of the year. These cells unite to form new colonies. Portuguese man-of-wars can live up to ten years but are often eaten by loggerhead turtles and other predators. Throughout the year, the prevailing winds blow them ashore on Atlantic coasts where they dry out in the warm sun.

THREAT: Changing ocean conditions

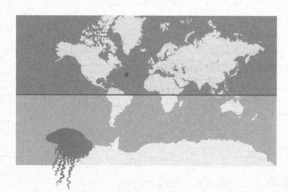

The strong winds blowing across the ocean strand thousands of Portuguese man-of-wars ashore.

NORTHERN HEMISPHERE

CONSERVATION STATUS: LC

Some animals live and travel in large groups for safety. Thousands of others are brought together by ocean currents. In either case, their numbers make them an awesome sight, helping to keep some animals away or attract others.

SPRINGBOK
(SOUTH AFRICA)

Between April and September, during the dry season, male springbok gather and guard groups of females until the females are ready to mate. There is a lot of fighting among males at this time, as well as "pronking." While pronking, adult springbok jump high with their backs arched and the white crest of hair raised. Pronking also happens when a springbok is threatened. During the rainy season, from October to November, females give birth to a single fawn. They are hidden in the grass for two weeks while their mother grazes nearby. The fawns suckle for many months, and by the time they are three or four weeks old, they spend most of their time with their mother's herd. Adult springbok prefer to feed on grass and leaves but will also eat shrubs, seeds, and flowers.

THREAT: *Not threatened, population increasing*

Jumping up—pronking—is a good way to warn other springbok to look out for danger.

SOUTHERN HEMISPHERE

Male springbok pronk even more in breeding season to show off how fit they are.

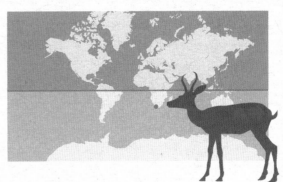

CONSERVATION STATUS: LC

MIGRATION

MONARCH BUTTERFLY

(NORTH AMERICA)

Monarch butterflies are unable to survive northern winters, so in the fall they migrate south in one long journey, feeding by day on flower nectar and resting at night. Arriving in their winter habitat, tens of thousands cluster on trees that have been used by generations of monarchs. In spring, the monarchs begin their journey north to lay eggs on milkweed. A few days after being laid, eggs will hatch into caterpillars and feed on milkweed. This diet gives caterpillars a bitter taste that deters predators even after metamorphosis. The caterpillar then molts into a chrysalis and, eight to fifteen days later, emerges a butterfly. The first three generations will survive only up to six weeks while they reproduce and continue north. The fourth generation will live six to eight months until they're ready to begin the process all over again.

THREATS: Climate change, habitat loss, herbicides

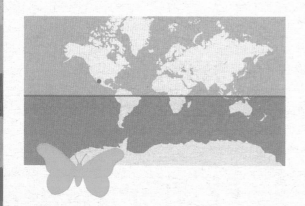

Huge flocks of monarch butterflies travel thousands of miles south to overwinter on trees in warmer climates.

NORTHERN HEMISPHERE

CONSERVATION STATUS: V

When temperatures begin to drop and food becomes scarce, some animals travel to warmer places to breed, often following routes that are repeated from generation to generation.

BAR-TAILED GODWIT
(AUSTRALIA AND NEW ZEALAND)

In October, around 155,000 very tired and hungry bar-tailed godwits collect on mudflats in Australia and New Zealand to feed. They have flown 7,500 miles (12,000 kilometers) nonstop from their breeding grounds in the Alaskan tundra, averaging 35 miles (60 kilometers) per hour. Their sleek feathers are designed for efficient flying, allowing the wind to pass easily over them. They congregate in flocks at high tide with other migratory birds. Probing the mud with their long bills, they dine on crustaceans, marine worms, and mollusks. By mid-March, they have doubled their body mass in preparation for their epic northern migration back to breeding grounds in the Alaskan tundra. There it will be spring, the ice will be thawing, and there will be plenty of food. Their babies are born, and they feast in preparation, once again, for their migration south.

THREATS: Habitat loss, rising sea levels, changing weather patterns

SOUTHERN HEMISPHERE

Under the right conditions, bar-tailed godwits depart New Zealand to fly thousands of miles to their breeding grounds on the Alaskan tundra.

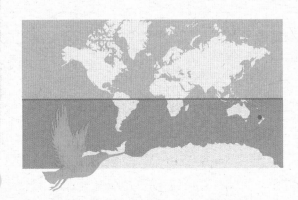

CONSERVATION STATUS: V

SAVE IT FOR LATER

HAZEL DORMOUSE
(SOUTHERN ENGLAND & WALES)

As temperatures begin to drop in late fall, dormice go into hibernation in nests made from tightly wound grass and hazel leaves. They hibernate all winter under leaves or logs, at the bases of trees, or just below the ground. As spring warms up, dormice emerge at night to eat insects and catkins, buds and flowers. Dormice can spend half of their lives sleeping. In spring, they will mate, and three or four weeks later, the female will give birth to an average of four babies. Only the mother looks after the young, who stay with her in the nest for one month and are independent after six to eight weeks. If food is abundant that summer, the female will produce another litter. The last of the litters are born in October. In the fall, the dormice fatten up on hazelnuts, fruit, and seeds to get ready for hibernation.

THREATS: Human behaviors causing loss of habitat

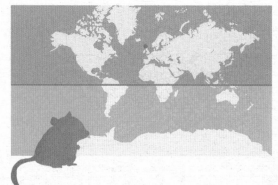

The dormouse lives for about five years. Curled up in a ball, it is now in its deepest sleep. It will sleep for half of its life.

NORTHERN HEMISPHERE

CONSERVATION STATUS: V

Some animals store energy in order to survive, adjusting to cold weather by going into hibernation, an inactive state resembling sleep. Other animals are biologically built to store food for times of crisis.

In the deserts of Western Australia, some honeypot ants have a special role as food larders. During the flowering season, they gorge on nectar so their bellies swell up like balloons.

SOUTHERN HEMISPHERE

HONEYPOT ANT
(AUSTRALIA)

The rainy season in some deserts of Australia yields plenty of food. Dead insects and nectar from desert plants are food for "repletes"—honeypot ants who store honey for their colony. They hang with full bellies from ceilings of nests dug deep into the cool earth and are fed mouth-to-mouth, drop-by-drop, by worker ants. During the dry season, when food is scarce, worker honeypot ants stroke the repletes' antennae, a signal to regurgitate the stored liquid. A worker may eat the liquid itself or carry it to another ant. There is one queen per colony and she may live eleven years, laying up to 1,500 eggs per day. Honeypot ants are part of the diet of some Indigenous Australians, who scrape the surface of the ground to locate the ant tunnels. They dig as deep as 7 feet (2 meters) to find the honeypots.

THREAT: Not threatened

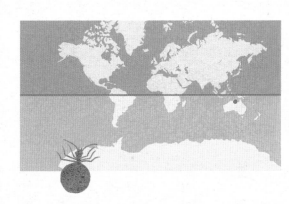

CONSERVATION STATUS: LC

THE SEARCH FOR FOOD

SNOW LEOPARD
(CENTRAL ASIA)

The snow leopards of Central Asia live in high mountain ranges such as the Himalayas. In winter, when they move to lower, slightly warmer areas following their prey, their large paws act like snowshoes and stop them from sinking into the snow. Moving daily from one spot to another, they change their home territory every few weeks to find food. In December and January, the usually solitary snow leopard pairs up to mate. Three to four months later, the female lines a nest in her den with her underbelly fur and gives birth to an average of two to three cubs. She keeps them warm by wrapping her huge tail around them. At two months old, they are still nursing but have also started eating food. At three months, they learn to hunt with their mother, catching marmots, mouse deer, blue sheep, and wild goats. In summer, they migrate 20,000 feet (6,000 meters) above sea level to the mountains.

THREATS: Habitat loss, poaching, decline in prey numbers

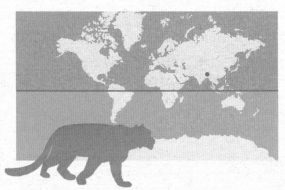

NORTHERN HEMISPHERE

In South Africa, the matriarch elephant leads her herd to lush new pastures as the five-month rainy season starts.

CONSERVATION STATUS:　V

The changing seasons often trigger the need for animals to be on the move to follow their food supply and to find new hunting grounds.

In Central Asia, the harsh winter brings the snow leopard down from the high rocky outcrops to the steep valleys below to feed.

SOUTHERN HEMISPHERE

AFRICAN ELEPHANT

(SOUTHERN AFRICA)

During the rainy season in Botswana, elephants congregate at flooded wetlands. It's a good time to breed, and bulls compete with one another to win a female. After about twenty-two months of pregnancy, a calf is born. Each herd is made up of mothers, their young, sisters, and cousins, all led by an older, wiser female matriarch. The herd helps to look after the young. When food is plentiful, they will travel about 1 mile (1.5 kilometers) each day. When it is scarce, they may travel up to 60 miles (100 kilometers). Elephants eat for most of the day, drink about 50 gallons (190 liters) of water, and average only two hours of sleep. In the dry season, they start their long trek to find fresh water, traveling single file down well-worn paths, with young elephants sometimes holding the tail in front with their trunk.

THREATS: Poaching, habitat loss, contact with humans

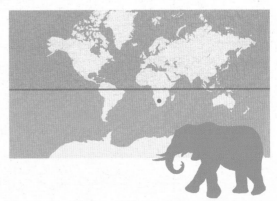

CONSERVATION STATUS: E

GLOSSARY

antennae ....long, thin sensory appendages found in pairs on the heads of insects

aquatic ....living in or near water

Arctic ....the region near the North Pole

behavior ....the way in which an organism responds to a situation or stimuli

body mass ....the total amount of matter that makes up an animal

camouflage ....a color or pattern on skin, scales, feathers, or leaves that helps something blend into the background

carapace......................a shell covering some or all of an animal's back

catkin ....a spike-like flower with no petals

chrysalis ....an inactive insect pupa, especially of a butterfly or moth

climate change ....the heating of the planet's atmosphere caused by an increase in greenhouse gases

clutch ....a group of eggs produced at a single time

colony ....a community of animals of one kind living close together

courtship ....the process in which animals and birds attempt to attract a mate for breeding

crèche ....a group of young animals cared for by adults

crustaceans ....a large group of mostly aquatic creatures including crabs, lobsters, shrimp, and barnacles

digestive system ....the part of the body that is involved in the process of digesting food

endangered ....in danger of becoming extinct as a species

environment ....the surroundings or conditions in which an organism lives

exoskeleton ....an external skeleton or protective covering, such as the shell of a snail

extreme conditions ..very severe weather

feeding grounds ....places where animals gather to find food

fermented ....having undergone chemical breakdown by bacteria or microorganisms

float ....a projection full of gas used to achieve buoyancy in water

fungi ....a large group of spore-producing organisms that feed on organic matter, including molds, yeasts, mushrooms, and toadstools

gland ....an organ of the body that secretes particular chemical substances

globe.............................the earth

grazes............................feeds on grass

habitat...........................the area where an organism naturally lives

hatchling ....a young animal just out of its egg

hibernation ....when an animal spends the winter in a dormant state

incubation ....when eggs are kept warm until they hatch

jostling ....pushing or bumping roughly

juveniles ....young animals

kits ....young beavers

larder ....area for storing food

larvae.............................the young of insects that later develop into other forms, such as caterpillars, butterflies, moths, and worms

leveret ....a young hare in its first year

life cycle ....the series of changes in the life of an organism, including reproduction

litter ....a number of young born to an animal at one time

lodge ....a beaver's den

matriarch ....the female head of a family

metamorphosis ....the process of transformation from an immature form to an adult form in two or more distinct stages

migration ....movement from one place to another

mimic ....to copy or take on the appearance of another thing, often in order to deter predators

mollusk ....a soft-bodied unsegmented animal with a shell

monsoon ....a strong seasonal wind that brings heavy rainfall

mound ....a raised mass of earth or similarly compacted material

mudflat ....a stretch of muddy land left uncovered at low tide

nursing ....when a young animal drinks milk from its mother's teats

outcrop ....a rock formation on the land surface

overwinter ....to spend the winter

performance ....a display of exaggerated behavior

poaching ....the illegal hunting or capturing of wild animals

predators ....animals that hunt other animals for food

pregnant ....carrying fertilized eggs or young before giving birth or laying eggs

prey ....animals eaten by other animals

probe ....to poke in order to explore

red milk ....a reddish-pink substance secreted by flamingos to feed to their young

region ....an area of a country or the world with particular characteristics, but not necessarily fixed boundaries

regurgitate ....to bring swallowed food back up into the mouth

reproductive cells ......female eggs and male sperm

reserves ....stores of food kept for later use

ritual ....a ceremony or performance

scarce ....rare

shimmying ....shaking or vibrating

sieve ....to strain solids from liquids

smuggling ....illegally transporting and selling

sociable ....engaging readily with others

soda lake ....a lake with a high level of sodium carbonate, which is responsible for the alkalinity of the water. A soda lake may also contain a high concentration of sodium chloride and other salts, making it saline.

specialized ....serving a specific function

stable ....firmly fixed

stoat ....a small carnivore of the weasel family

subtropical ....bordering on the tropics

suckle ....to feed from the breast or teat

territory ....the area a creature treats as its home ground

tundra ....treeless plains in the Arctic regions of the Northern Hemisphere

wean ....to take a baby off its mother's milk and put it onto solid foods

INDEX

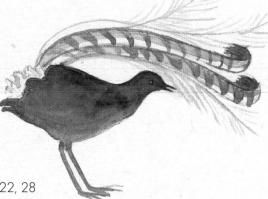

EXTRA INFORMATION

FURTHER READING

There are many reference books available on wildlife, but sometimes it's good to look up information on the internet. You will need to be sure your internet sources are reliable, with accurate facts. Here are a few useful websites.

https://animaldiversity.org
https://www.britannica.com
https://www.iucn.org/resources/conservation-tools/iucn-red-list-threatened-species
https://www.nationalgeographic.com

HOW YOU CAN HELP

Here are some ways that you can help our wildlife and combat climate change:

- Research climate change and endangered species.
- Contact politicians and ask them to take action against climate change and reduce the use of fossil fuels.
- Tell your family and friends about climate change and conservation.
- Reduce your use of plastic and recycle as much as you can, don't litter, and turn off lights and electrical appliances.
- Eat less meat and more veggies.
- Walk or cycle rather than take the car and reduce your air travel.

- Buy secondhand products or those made from sustainable resources.
- Make your garden wildlife-friendly by planting natives, keeping your cat indoors, and putting out water for native animals.
- Don't waste food or water.

Greenland

Alaska
(US)

Canada

North
America

North
Atlantic
Ocean

United States of America

Mexico

Bahamas

Cuba

Dominican Republic

Belize   Haiti
Guatemala   Honduras

Central   El Salvador   Nicaragua
America   Costa Rica

Panama   Guyana
Venezuala   Suriname

Colombia   French Guiana

Ecuador

Peru   Brazil

Bolivia

Paraguay

South
America   Uruguay

Chile   Argentina

N

W   E

S